Living Proof

for Roy McTarnaghan,
with thanks,
[signature] '75
1989

Living Proof

Poems by
Edmund Skellings

UNIVERSITY PRESSES OF FLORIDA
Florida International University Press
Miami

OF these poems, only "Florida" has appeared
previously, printed as a poster in *Geojourney,* a
publication of the State of Florida Department
of Natural Resources.

Library of Congress Cataloging in Publication Data

Skellings, Edmund
  Living proof.

  I. Title.
PS 3537.K33L5   1985   811'.54   86-19123

ISBN 0-8130-0857-3 (alk. paper)

UNIVERSITY PRESSES OF FLORIDA, the agency of
the State of Florida's university system for the
publication of scholarly and creative works,
operates under policies adopted by the Board
of Regents. Its offices are located at
15 Northwest 15th Street, Gainesville, Florida
32603.

To my dear friends
Gregory and Mary Ann Wolfe,
living proof of the arts and the graces.

Contents

Ocean

The gray falls down to green. The line
Of sky is dimming. Lights
Bob up curve down curve up. The
Self dips. We
Are stars at sea
Swimming.

Opening Poem

The first poem in the book should be
The best poem in the book and we
Better be brought up to snuff.
No fooling. Give us
The crack shot, top measure,
No dandelion on the lawn.

Each line should snap like a spinnaker
Or a noose. Nothing halfway.
Mother should peer out at us.
We ought not be able to finish it
Without glancing around
Or shifting our seat.

The whole wash should hang out heavy,
The sun should glare hot on it,
We should smell the damp in our breath,
Color should bloom like a flowerbed,
And we should know with pure faith
Life will whip in the wind by afternoon.

Vincent, Vincent

The green blue walls open wide
Like a book. The red brown floor
Tiles fall like a sprung trap door.
The sunflower chair is hurled at you.
Its color held him like a bee.

All day his brain turned slowly with the sun.
He sat silent as Midas. Even
The hot French wind on his face was yellow.
No wonder he got lost in a starry night. But
That chair is carved from flower stuff.

Gold enough, gold enough.

Paul Gauguin

I know why you had to leave. He
Loved you, but saw through everything.
He was so alone, except for God shining down,
The need for man was utter. Side by side,
Scene by scene, you were becoming a vanishing

Point. And then the second chair: all that
Evident love in the curve and the color. So much so
You lost you, sailing away for your dear life, but
Dear Paul, your absence fills that empty chair,
While deep in your green jungle,

His eye is the leopard's eye.

Ages

It was Louis Pasteur, I believe,
Who wasted almost one year
With his eye to a powerful lens
Trained on a little dish.

With a needle he moved a powder:
All the righthanded crystals left,
All the lefthanded crystals right,
Two tiny teaspoons of crystals.

Imagine him there, scarcely breathing,
Not a feather of wind in the room,
Teasing his crystals with needles
Into two tiny peaks on the dish.

It took him almost a year,
Student Pasteur with his needles.
And then, of course, the announcement
For which, of course, no one waited:

All living crystals are
Righthanded crystals. And
Righthanded crystals only.
The rest of the universe
Mixes its crystals. Life

Is righthanded, righthanded.

That experiment now is buried
Under the dust of the thousands
Of long dull laboratory hours,
Most of them yielding no answers,
Or, what is worse, no questions.

It is all a matter of finding.
Or not finding. No one remembers
The aching neck of young Louis
Holding his breath in a room,
Holding his fingers so steady,

In an Age when, we say, life was slower.

Black Hole

—for Stephen Hawking

You remind me of a curious vine.
No matter what, it grew as it grew
And played itself out lightward,
Climbing up and upon some lack.

By twining about an absence,
It raised a green question
As a flute will a cobra.

So your song curls around silence:
Either nothing is right there or
Something is not right there.

If I could code precise words
To what I am surely not saying,
We would fathom the utter darkness
Between fact and fact, but

My figure is easy as your figure:
Aside from the sense of humor,
There is absolutely nothing to it.

Robert Frost

He held himself apart until the man
Was the last rustic. Rockers creak
When you read him, boulders balance.

The final lines of his poems
Fall like an avalanche, seen
With the sound turned down.

We turn down sound.
We turn down poets and their lives.

I put the complete poems back on the shelf to yellow
Like a sheaf of pressed

Flowers from another summer,
Index my spectacles,

And peer again at the computer
Screen. The color words are flying like
A flock of butterflies on a mown field.

Men work together, I tell him from the heart,
Whether they work together,
Or apart.

Chicopee River

There is no reason
Why this memory
Should open like a yellow umbrella
Dry in the downpour,

But I am there, a boy
Sliding the hundreds of feet
Down the hot sand banks of the Chicopee
Where they shine in the summer's sun
Like the top half of a huge
Hourglass.

Young, I am young,
And I rush with the young down
Long rides upon the cardboard sleds.
I can even see close
My worn-through canvas shoes.

Fifty does that. More
And more, old times are clear as
Magnified print, while

The moments of today
Drop like the coins
Of a boy with a hole
In his pocket.

It is pouring and pouring here,
Hard as sand from a shoe.

I shall hold tight to this desk,
As we fly fast as a dream
From moment to moment to moment
Back up the quicksilver river
Even as far as Indian Bend.

My mother is there.
And my father.

Living and living and living.

Prayer

Like it or not,
We like our wild things in a pot.

We turn the green face from the sun
For symmetry, we say, for
Balance. One

Skeptic might suspect
Another simple need of Man
For order in the growth of God.

We trim the sod, we clip
Clip the bushes, underlining that the tree
In truth knows East and West
As well as we.

And it tastes darkness at the root.
And at the leaf the sunny absolute.

Oh God who turns my mind first
This then that
Way, please

Give me my bright way. For I
(And certainly it is my doom)
Feel a short quarter-inch from
(May I call it)

Bloom?

Artificial Intelligence

Euclid rolled over in his bones
When Newell & Simon instructed
Their machine to look for new proof
For bisecting the ordinary triangle.

No one at all expected
Except perhaps Newell & Simon
The machine to say something unheard of.

But it did. And there
Was the glorious proof, never dreamed
By any mathematician, but
I ask you, Newell & Simon,

How can any imagine that somewhere
Inside a triangle turned
Over, one side as a hinge?
Or was there even a triangle?
Or even a line or a point?
Or even a sharpened formula?
Or even the thought of a shape?

Was there any joy in the crystals?
Any Aha or Eureka?
How sad, Misters Newell & Simon,
That no one awoke in a sweat,
Making inherent coherent,
So the living are left to explain
How an inanimate universe
Can contrive to make itself plain.

Words for Jesus of Nazareth

I

My heart hangs
Hangs on a curve between two beating pains
Slung in a red hammock
Tossing in dreams of a future

I know I am a man
To breathe is to crush the heart

Spittle runs from the eyebrow
Down the cheek to the beard
Cold trace

I know I am a man the nails
Divining rods

The penis a crushed ache
Up from
I know I am a man
The fear behind their faces
In their whips
Hangs

Too long
Pray

II

Hums rise
Light rises

Dark the wet womb

And the great stone of birth to roll back

III

Heaven the unblemished manhood

IV

The smooth cool wood I remember
Oil sliding my palm on the shine
The shavings of sweet freshness

And the call away I remember

The long life of tasks
The clear image of fate in the well

Water for the desert
Kisses for the lepers

V

I know I am a man

Hung

Up

Side

Down

Florida

We are South looking North.
Or vice versa.
We are international
And exceptionally local.

From here you could go to the moon.
And we can prove it.

Even the natives are transients.
Arriving and departing,
We are of two minds.

Coast to coast here means
One hour through our cotton mountains.
The sun rises and sets under salt waters.

Knowing in the bones that space is time,
We are wise as any peninsula.
We mine the dried beds of forgotten seas.
Fresh mango and orange bloom from the silt.

Outside Gainesville once, I reached down
Into time and touched the saber tooth of a tiger.
No atlas prepared me for the moist
Sweet smell of his old life.

Suddenly a flock of flamingos
Posed a thousand questions,
Blushing like innocence.

But the moon, perfectly above Miami
Like some great town clock, whispers,
"Now . . . yesterdays . . . tomorrows . . ."

And standing tropically and hugely still
At this port of meditation,
Reduced to neither coming nor going,
We are together on the way to somewhere.

In good time.

Tutankhamen Traveling

With no perspective, I sit like the true Egyptian.
Flat, I am become the scene and the wall.
As far as your curved eye can see,
Thousands of me line the hall.

And I ask you what you expected to find:
Was it the round earth or the round mind?

My world is infinitely open forever.
My journey never ends. Nothing ever returns
Upon itself. The white clouds sail the blue,
The blue, forming the blue, vanishing,

Suddenly it is raining everywhere at once.
There is never anything but now going on.

Tell me, shall my mask speak golden truths?
Tell me, where will you leave your face?

I shall always sit in a spectacular desert,
My civilization about me like a cloak.

Gulliver

The nostril was familiar
Long grey hair curling out and away
Then the wart on the cheek next to the wrinkle
He knew it then

His face it was he crawled
Could feel the tickle looked down
There he was near the wart and wrinkle

How could this be
Finding oneself sticky with satire
Lessened and lessoned

Own features blown
Heady with headings

The answer came searching and found him
Empuzzled

Time upon time the most super imposure
Face after face mirror on mirror

Math after math after math after math

Poem for Wyatt Wyatt

Satan,
Having mulled things over
In a frigid clime,
Had decided that next time
(And make no mistake about it)
He was gonna get God good.

Having bided,
Opportunity knocked its once
And God went down
Past absolute zero
To where he belonged,
As Satan put it.

We all make mistakes,
Said God, departing heaven,
But before the Devil
Had counted to, say, seven,

God's GOD appeared
In a puff of red plasma gas,
Saying to Satan,
Not bad, but . . .

Your idea of heaven is not the last
Idea of heaven.

Janice

If she were a goddess and we told her story
We would say Death had fallen in love
And reaching around to hold her close
One of his powerful fingers had slipped in.

The cancer they took out from her back
Looked like a finger the doctor agreed
Though he had to send away for a name
To discover whether the touch was malign.

She must wait a week and we must wait a week
To find in a message from a white laboratory
If that fellow's intentions are sincere
And how the family will act if he asks her hand.

Morning

The local priest floats by in his blue car.
He is in no hurry and the radio is on loud.
He, for one, has never done one thing wrong.
He is in heaven already. Life is a long ritual.

Meanwhile, on the porch screened against flies,
This poet sits biting his quick, sipping caffeine,
Smoking one cigar after another. Smoky as Hell.
Life to him scarcely makes anything out clearly.

The moral is, and everything either has or hasn't
A moral, the moral is, count your blessings
Without anyone watching. And on your knees.
Hell is waiting for everyone who sits too easy.

Florida Turnpike

Green scrub plain against a cyan sky,
White clouds, white highway, and
You began to sing, Eubie Blake,
Of yourself and your shadow
And that avenue in New York.

Now you are a shade, Eubie,
Even your notes fall on my ears
Like little bird shadows

In the elevator, out of hearing of
Joe Franklin and the camera,
You extended those long black fingers,
Made chords in the air,
And gave me an eighty-year-old wink,
Saying, "Just me
And my shadow."

You are gone, Eubie Blake.
I am your shadow.

Memo of Compliance

—for Steve Altman

Yes, yes, yes, another report
Of how I am fulfilling something
Or other: please believe, I mean
No disrespect, but these people
I have been sent among. Their
Alphabet is odd. Their God,
Even, I cannot understand.

Christ, in fact, any Messiah,
Is so far from their understanding
(Or their wish) . . .

I would you knew them as I
Try to know them, Barbarians
Is not even apt. They seem
To worship. They seem to
Pray. But I cannot keep
Even close to accurate accounts
Of what I have done, accomplished,
Or what I intend to do
Tomorrow, if I have the chance.

I know you need some justification
Of why I have been sent here,
Some rationale of your position
Keeping me on . . . I'm at a loss
To answer more than that I try,

Or hope to try, or plan, perhaps,
To start to try, or learn to
Begin to try . . . harder? (Is that
What you want, or think you want,
From me, or what I was, at least?)
Or shrewder, or more successfully?
I do keep up. Some days I don't know
What I keep. Barbarians, I said.
It's not just that. They seem
To have a culture all their own.
Values, maybe. Or maybe what
We imagine are values.

I need . . . vacation? I am already
Vacant in some ways. Write me,
Please. But no more reports,
Understand, or be prepared for
Suspicions of what I do, or
Might do. Believe the rumors.
I am doing everything imaginable
To sustain myself. And you.
Whoever I am. Or you are.
Best. Sincerely. Yours.
Respectfully, whatever that means.

Key Largo

It is nothing like the movie.
No one here bets the horses,
Certainly not Fancy Free.

Even the slow long-bladed fans
Are gone. Only champagne and pompano
Still go together.

In the rest of the country, well.
Rocco still runs things.
We still count the votes
Until they come out right.

As Bogey says, he was just
Passing through.

Time Study

—for Romeo Skellings

Romeo would stopwatch Love,
The Night Super was fond of saying.
But my father went clicking along,
Charting the motions of manufacture,
And one day a man from the government
Raised a blue flag with a golden E.
There was a short ceremony
And then they went back to war.

I have mused about this at some
Length, studying how to get
Idea in fit words, whether or when
I could sneak a smoke in the Men's room.

Most of my friends go leisurely about
Inattentive to the Efficiency of Nature,
So you see it does pose a problem.
Should one do this or that first?
Can one eliminate waste
Movements of the mind in the maze?
When is good enough toward perfection?

He is with me always, frowning Not Bad, Not
Bad. Yeats is there, too, the two
Conniving geezers worrying if
My last word has a well quit snap.

Her Class Reunion

—for Lolita Skellings

So little history is ever set
In the bold black and white of books.

Sigh for the moments never set down,
Sigh for the moments almost forgotten.

It is like coming suddenly from the hot sun
Into the cool of the bookstore, browsing,
Turning the pages of a strange history,
Coming upon your own face in an old photo.

I didn't remember I was there! Look, there's . . .
What was his name? And her, now. Remember?

It is like coming from the hot sun of today
Into the cool book of history. Can it be
That long ago? Listen! Fifty years
Is the hinge of the Century. Soon its
Great door will close, so,

Open the pages, quick, open them wide,

(For the children only learn of generals
And presidents, of battlefield and marketplace,
Years reduced to numbers . . .)

Open the real history. See? We are there,
Walking quietly home from school,
Waving to friends,
Waiting for trolleys,
Admiring the new car, and the talk, remember?
Remember those long fast hours
In the green shade of the trees?

(And the children, bored, can shut our book,
And we can shut our book, take the deep breath
Of Tomorrow . . .)

But we were together.
And we are again together.
And we will always be together.

The Bells

—for Harold and
Constance Crosby

Gathered here, we make a church.

And something in the memory
Rhymes. Remember

Leaping upon the air, the long
Slow pull upon the rope, the give
And fall. Our bodies

Brought down tones upon the town.

Now these two bells.
These two bells here
In tune in time.

Oh, leap upon the air, for
To tune two bells against the din
And clamor of our everydays,

Each ringer, chimer, rhymer, tells
The toll. But toils. And tolls.

We sound against the dark, against
Our fears, we sound

Not melody, but sympathy.

Oh, tones together, chime.
Above the warring of the sexes, chime.
Above the squabble of the nations, chime.

Oh love that rings above all time,
That makes time needless but to ring upon,
Tell One plus One

Be One.

Against that dark, against
Those fears, against all going, go
To bed for all of us tonight, tonight

And everynight. Oh,

Chime.

Courses

The rattan fan blades follow
Each other round and round and
Round and occasionally
I catch their drift.

They are something like my friends,
Stiff in their courses,
Circling one another,
Their innards are silent.

Their intent is imperceptible:
Lazily hypnotic, crazily repetitive,
One could grow quite mad guessing
What grand hyperbolas
Those blades might follow

If all power and all hell
Broke loose.

Commune

Spread eagle back upon the waters of the bed,
My love afloat under an arm with lost feeling,
Cedar planks and cedar beams and the slow
Revolve of the bright blades of the brass fan,

My eyes through the twin sky-lights
Upon the lit white clouds
Upon a night of space
And then the moon, cratered with time . . .

Star fish. I am a star fish flung . . .

And you said,
"What are you thinking?"

Eye Teeth

At the bell I bring my bag of sweets
And open the door to a flock of ghosts.
One particular black vampire sneers,
Showing formidable green wax fangs.
I smile. Good show. They each select
A Milky Way. I make them take a tangerine.

The ghosts vanish into the night. I sit,
Awaiting the next set of ghouls, sucking
My hard candy. Last Hallowed Eve
The fiends were at the door for hours,
More frightening than they knew,
Caricatures of our bestial past,
Funny displays of instinct.

I looked up at a Palm Beach dinner once,
Thinking of nothing except cutlery and
All were showing their teeth with smiles
And biting down on flesh and chewing.
The expensive veneer of civilization
Fell away, then, and I swigged the white wine.

Get away from the door, goblins, scat
Skeletons, back back back black witches.
You can't turn unreal what I know is real.
I go to the plain unenchanted mirror.
The ghosts of all my ancestors look back.

Statuesque

I have been an inhabitor of statues,
That strange disease of looking
Through their patient eyes.

From Rushmore I gaze, and out
Sphinxish, on the blank sand.

Deep, under the sea called
Mediterranean, I am the silent
Christ of the Abysses, blessing
The deaths of divers.

High in the Andes, I look out
Over the bay of Rio.

Horses leap under me. Great
Snakes battle my muscles.
I am beautiful as Adonis.

Translated into marble,
I will live forever.

Vocals

Cats cry like babies to get a pet.
Dog mimicks dog to bark think twice.
Bears rumble growls to fur the cave.
Wolves howl solace across the ice.

Words that fit so well are few.
When you cried today, I cried too.

Free Climbing

By fifty-three one ought to be depressed.
I got it over with by forty. Doc said,
Sounds as if you yearn for Mount Olympus.

Damn tooting. I soloed round the lesser stones:
Deborah, Hess, Hayes, even McKinley,
Stared in a green glacier a million years.

Settling for pebbles after is demeaning,
Might as well go to the nearest moon.
I shuddered off both doctor and depression,

So in my sixties I'd be elevated
As well as get, somehow someway by Jove,
That god damned rocky mountain recreated.

Clear Moon

Footprints on the moon are prints of feet
In the mind only. Much may be seen
By this method, my brothers, antique
Though it seem. Poets get deft
And half daft with such looking.

Youth may loom close this way,
Stay prepared for tears:
Summer lovers, sunshine friends,
The eye of the traitor before and after.

And take this warning from one well practiced:
Hindsight is foresight. Don't wander or

Look ahead like a greedy lizard,
Look back like a god on an ape.

Notes on Relative Inertia

And now too late as usual
The physics professor tells me
Everything depends on everything else.

For without the distant stars
Objects in motion would not (necessarily)
Remain in motion.

I would have to keep throwing the ball.
Nothing would fall. Push
Would come to shove.

There would be no rest for the wicked
Or anyone. No body could get on
In the world. Or any where.

Most likely in the next lesson
Where will go. If there is go.
So you and me love better make hay

While the sun shines.

News Brief

Nothing happened today. Yesterday
Sat like a pool ball rack. If
You were shocked by headline,
Stunned by photograph, electrified
By bloody details from the bandaged survivor,
Blame the loose set, damp chalk,
Bad cue, even the uneven table.

It wasn't your scratch. It wasn't
From your genes, nature, or nurture.
You were not odd. Blame it on God.

Driver Ed

Everyone pulls the shining colorfully painted
Automobile he paid an arm and a leg for
Over to the side of the road and then off the road
And leans the hot forehead against the cool steering wheel
Once in his young life.

                That's the last chapter, chum:
No sense turning back, no point pushing on.
And you are learning a lesson about the top speed of life
That none of the experts rushing by can help with.

Nuclear

The atom is not like a ring
Of marbles. No no, nor
Some great knuckler must
Be imagined, huge knees
Hunkered down. God's ass
In the air, eyes intent
On a smoky blue agate
Should not be thought of.

Nor the planets like
Oranges spinning in orbits
From jugglers, think upon.

For the mind will hunker down,
Then. Or spin.

Vision instead those old carved ivory
Chinese globes within globes
Within globes. Use your long
Fingernail to inspect the
Interiors. Latticed within
Lattice, so thin they are held
Together by their own holding.

The electron is nowhere. Rather
It is not anywhere, rather it is
Its shell, rather it is almost
A shell. Shell within shell
Whispers like a shoreline.
From shell to shell the
Shushing goes. Passage
Is all there is of is.

Gladiatorial

We, who are about to die, Caesar,
Salute you, because such is the nature
Of bureauracy, military or any other ary.
We know you enjoy the differential
Twixt physical deference and mental
Detestation. By Jupiter, you sure do get
Your toga up over similar tensions. We
Desire you lionized, but bow behind
Swords and nets. Plenipotentiaries, know this:
Half a chance, different birth, dice
In our favor, muscle would muscle flab, we'd
The gift of gab, ours the flag, the name,
The game. Meanwhile, we die for you over
The leftover, hank of zebra, leopard hair,
Meek to inherit the last hack of the earth.

Senior Citizen

My dad decided he would burn.
His buddies always said he would.
His tailor did him as he should
And hot flame fit him to a turn.

He's running rum or chasing fur
In heaven or perhaps in hell.
My father read dice as they fell.

Things were for him the way they are
And are tonight the way they were.
Fool fool, star star.
He always loved a bright red car.

What he lived was all he learned.
My dad decided to be burned.

Carnival

Your youth is an old slut, dumb,
She'll raise her skirts
For your quick look, but
It's the same ogle, buddy,
Want something wild? Want
Something crazy? Something . . .?

Ah, she goes through the motions,
The same old struts and bumps,
And it takes a jaded eye
To catch anything new. She's
Recalcitrant, puts out fake shy,
Then tells all to anybody.

You want to peek something novel,
Con her into a fresh attitude?
She's tired, yawns easy. You
Gonna pay through the nose
And the heart for a second ticket.

Love Song in Age

—for Philip Larkin

Love better not want no reward,
Said the old pimp looking back,
No John ever knew what I know,
No working stiff nor any man Jack,

And take this from a taker
Who never gave it free before,
Life has a last card up his sleeve
When you fall down for your old whore.

Down Home Question

Been gone a long time fella
Half the way to hell

Can ya tell me if my honey
Still carry water from the well

And if she carries water
Is there anyone long with her

Is there someone with that water
Goin home with her

Cause if there is ol fella
Cause if there is oh

Well whittle me a sharp stick
And push it in the sand

Tell her it hurt me that hard
When I am long and gone

Save it up till I'm out of sight
Then tell her all at once

Whittle it up stab it in the sand
Tell her all at once

Say I went the way to hell but
I'm still in love with her

46

No better not tell her that no
Just say you cant racall

And that I passed you straight on by
No dont say a word

Then none can say you lied old man
None can say you lied

But tell me if my honey
Carry water from the well

Tell me if my honey
Haul that water from the well

Down Home Answer

See by your eyes mister
You have had no home some time

See by your eyes mister
You knew our Emma Jean

And if you be her darlin
Id be for leavin town

For they found her floatin last year
Wearin her weddin gown

Now I am just an old man
Haveta pay no mind to me

But I wouldnt stay here long son
Even to go and see

Wave to me up the road a ways
She was my daughter see

Wave to me up the road son
She loved you more than me

But that girl was my daughter
And she was right by me

Now I got a lot of whittlin
To do before its dark

But I'll whittle you a heart shape
Out of the purest bark

And I'll lay it in her flowers
Lighter than any lark

She never held no grudges
And I'm not gonna start

You run off like her mama
So I'm not gonna start

But if you get to Natchez
Or even see the Nile

Think of here as home always
And remember her a while

Music

I

Whole notes and half notes, big and little birds
Make telephone wires a staff of melody.
Nearby, a full bush cackles at random.

What do I think? I think
The whole world musics this morning,
Ordered or zany, centered or wry,

And I think so long last night,
Far away tomorrow. Day is
Sky enough to hold the huge singing.

II

Your fingers go here on the flute.
The thumb goes there. Now get
That's right only the other
Thumb rests here with nothing to do.

If song were simple, I could
Get the grip, I could wrap
My hands any way round the breath.

But my fingers go here on the flute,
The typewriter, the gun. Practice
Makes imperfect, too. You can hear
The valves of the heart miss a stop.

Choochoo Train

How we
Oh how we
Oh woe how we
Woe how we
Howhow   howhow

Oh woe how we
Whowho
Oh woe

Loving Memory

I see it white tonight. I see Robert
At his door. I see the yellow flames
Of the tall candles burning halos
In the frosted windows. Robert Tucker,
Teacher at the door, you are New
England, all welcome from the cold.

Comic Poem

The G-men were ready
They knew that the crooks would
Snap at the bait

Hello Santucci
What can I do for you

Canayou use a some stuff

You are under arrest Santucci
I am a G-man

Ha ha onayou
I am a the C I A

Said the poet to his moll
Giggles

Sleight Of

Hey, here is the
Black silk top hat and
My hand reaches
Deep and by the long long ears pulls out

The white rabbit
You knew would happen out of force
Of habit.

But you fellow, readily deluded,
Wonder at this:

There is no rabbit no
Black silk ha ha top hat
And you and I are left with only these
Rapidly evaporating magic
Words.